LIFT EV'RY VOICE
AND SING

LIFT EV'RY VOICE AND SING

by *James Weldon Johnson*

Illustrated by Jan Spivey Gilchrist

SCHOLASTIC INC.
New York Toronto London Auckland Sydney

*Grateful acknowledgment to Rev. and Mrs. Cartwright and family
for their assistance.*

ISBN 0-590-46983-5

"Lift Ev'ry Voice and Sing" - James Weldon Johnson, J. Rosamond Johnson.
Used by permission of Edward B. Marks Music Company.
Illustrations copyright © 1995 by Jan Spivey Gilchrist.
All rights reserved. Published by
Scholastic Inc.

12 11 10 9   5 6 7 8 9/0

Printed in the U.S.A.   08

The paintings in this book were executed in
colored pencil, gouache, and watercolor.

Calligraphy by Jeanyee Wong

For ARTHUR *and* ANN EILAND,
with thanks for all you've done.
— *J.S.G.*

Lift ev'ry voice
and sing,
Till earth and
heaven ring,

Ring with the
harmonies of Liberty;

Let our rejoicing rise
High as the list'ning skies,

Let it resound loud as the rolling sea.

Sing a song full of the faith
      that the dark past has taught us;

Sing a song
full of the hope
that the present
has brought us;

Facing the rising sun
of our new day begun,
Let us march on
till victory is won.

Stony the road we trod,
Bitter the chast'ning rod,
Felt in the days when hope
unborn had died;

Yet with a steady beat,
Have not our weary feet

Come to the place for which
our fathers sighed?

We have come over a way
that with tears has been watered;
We have come, treading our path
thro' the blood of the slaughtered,

Out from the gloomy past.
Till now we stand at last
Where the white gleam of
our bright star is cast.

God of our weary years,
God of our silent tears,

Thou who hast brought us
thus far on the way;

Thou who hast by Thy might,
Led us into the light,

Keep us forever in the path,
we pray.

Lest our feet stray
from the places,
our God, where we met Thee,

Lest our hearts,
drunk with the wine of the world,
we forget Thee;

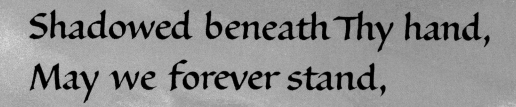

Shadowed beneath Thy hand,
May we forever stand,

True to our God,
      True to our native land.

LIFT EV'RY VOICE AND SING

Lyrics by JAMES WELDON JOHNSON

Music by J. ROSAMOND JOHNSON

Maestoso ben sostenuto

Lift ev - 'ry voice and sing, Till earth and heav - en
Ston - y the road we trod, Bit - ter the chast - 'ning
God of our wear - y years, God of our si - lent

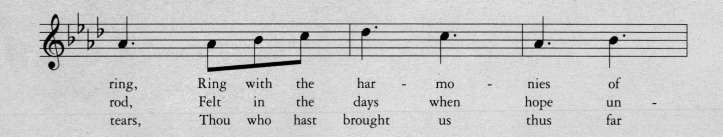

ring, Ring with the har - mo - nies of
rod, Felt in the days when hope un -
tears, Thou who hast brought us thus far

Lib - er - ty; Let our re - joic - ing
born_____ had died; Yet with a stead - y
on_____ the way; Thou who hast by Thy

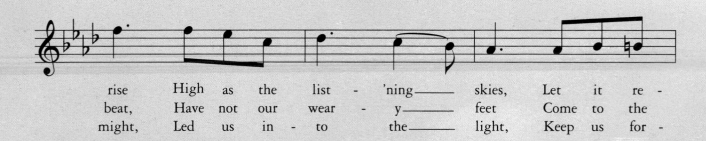

rise High as the list - 'ning_____ skies, Let it re -
beat, Have not our wear - y_____ feet Come to the
might, Led us in - to the_____ light, Keep us for -

sound loud as the roll - ing sea.
place for which our fa - thers sighed?
ev - er in the path, we pray.

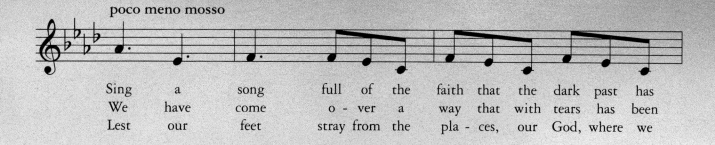

poco meno mosso

Sing a song full of the faith that the dark past has
We have come o - ver a way that with tears has been
Lest our feet stray from the pla - ces, our God, where we

poco a poco rall.

taught us; Sing a song full of the
wa - tered; We have come, tread - ing our
met Thee, Lest our hearts, drunk with the

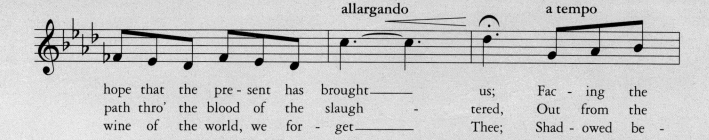

allargando   **a tempo**

hope that the pre - sent has brought—————— us; Fac - ing the
path thro' the blood of the slaugh - tered, Out from the
wine of the world, we for - get—————— Thee; Shad - owed be -

ris - ing sun of our new day be -
gloom - y past. Till now we stand at————
neath Thy hand, May we for - ev - er————

gun, Let us march on till vic - to - ry———— is won.
last Where the white gleam of our bright star———— is cast.
stand, True to our God, True to our na - tive land.

DEAR READERS,

Have you ever watched a sunset in silence? Did you hear music rising and falling as the colors changed — music that was loud and strong, soft and gentle, music that lasted until the sun had set?

When I was a young girl, I heard the music. I wanted to hear it also in my art. I wanted to paint the music I heard in sunsets, in the faces of loved ones and friends, and, especially, in the faces of children. I wanted to paint not just what was easy to see, but what existed beneath the surface; to paint not just the eyes, but the sparkle in them. I wanted to paint the power, the strength, and the beauty in life.

The people of Africa, such as the Maasai of the East pictured in these illustrations, have also heard the music. They believe that children are the most precious of nature's gifts. And they are right.

J. Rosamond Johnson heard the music, too, along with his brother, the poet and educator James Weldon Johnson, the man who wrote such stirring words for the love of his children:

Lift ev'ry voice and sing,

Till earth and heaven ring, . . .

Mr. Johnson heard the power of children lifting themselves up, moving forward, and, always, marching ahead: sometimes loud and strong; sometimes soft and gentle.

I hope this book will reflect the greatness we have seen and heard in your eyes, like a mirror, not of glass, but of water: a living, breathing reflection, moving forward, *always*.

Jan Spivey Gilchrist